# Post-Traumatic Stress Disorder in Children

LIVERPOOL
JOHN MOORES UNIVERSITY
AVRIL ROBARTS LRC
TITHEBARN STREET
LIVERPOOL L2 2ER
TEL. 0151 231 4022

Books are to be returned on or before
the last date below.

D0569085

LIVERPOOL JMU LIBRARY

3  1111  00735 8516

The PACTS series: *Parent, Adolescent and Child Training Skills*

# Post-Traumatic Stress Disorder in Children

*by*
Martin Herbert

BPS BOOKS  THE BRITISH PSYCHOLOGICAL SOCIETY

First published in 1996 by BPS Books (The British Psychological Society), St Andrews House, 48 Princess Road East, Leicester LE1 7DR, UK.

© Martin Herbert, 1996

This book is sold subject to the condition that it shall not, by way of trade or otherwise, be lent, resold, hired out, or otherwise circulated without the publisher's prior consent in any form of binding or cover other than that in which it is published and without a similar condition including this condition imposed on the subsequent purchaser.

A catalogue record for this book is available from the British Library.

ISBN 1 85433 197 3

Whilst every effort has been made to ensure the accuracy of the contents of this publication, the publishers and author expressly disclaim responsibility in law for negligence or any other cause of action whatsoever.

Typeset by Ralph Footring, Derby.

Printed in Great Britain by Stanley L. Hunt Printers Ltd., Rushden, Northants.

# Contents

APPENDIXES

HINTS FOR PARENTS

# Post-traumatic stress disorder in children

> *Deep, unspeakable suffering may well be called a baptism, a regeneration,*
> *the initiation into a new state.*
>
> George Eliot: *Adam Bede* (1859)

## Introduction

### Aims

The aim of this guide is to provide practitioners with a brief introduction to the clinical management of Post-Traumatic Stress Disorder (PTSD) in Children. This will include a description of the disorder; an account of the shortcomings of the diagnosis; guidelines for treating/counselling children suffering from PTSD; and a checklist for assessing PTSD.

Following major emotional or physical upheavals such as disasters, accidents or bereavement, a high proportion of children experience several distressing reactions including anxiety, fear and depression. It is now acknowledged that many actually manifest symptoms of Post Traumatic Stress Disorder (PTSD), and that without treatment their disorder can persist over long periods of time.

The diagnostic category of post-traumatic stress disorder in adults has only been acknowledged since the publication of the third edition of the American Psychiatric Association's *Diagnostic and Statistical Manual* (DSM-III) in 1980, and thus the use of the specific term PTSD is, relatively speaking, in its infancy. Of late, the fourth edition of the *Diagnostic and Statistical Manual* (DSM-IV), and *World Health Organisation* classification, 10th edition (ICD-10), have both come to recognize that children suffer from PTSD (see *Appendix I*).

### Objectives

After studying the guide you should be able:

1. to describe and recognize Post-Traumatic Stress Disorder (PTSD) in children;

2.    to answer parents' questions about the disorder and its conse-
      quences;
3.    to conduct a preliminary assessment of PTSD;
4.    to be familiar with therapeutic strategies used in dealing with these
      consequences;
5.    to be aware of some of the shortcomings in our knowledge base
      relating to this problem;
6.    to further your reading of the literature beyond the brief account
      provided in this guide.

## The development of the concept PTSD

Yule (1994) in a comprehensive account of PTSD traces the history
of the disorder as it emerged in the psychiatric literature as a separate
condition rather than a variant of other well-recognized problems
such as anxiety, phobias or depression. He points out how the concept
of PTSD was first developed in relation to studies of adult reactions
to major stress, notably the 'shell shock' or 'battle fatigue' suffered
by servicemen and women in two World Wars, and more recently
the Vietnam War. The dramatic and long-lasting psychological effects
of battle for many individuals came to be seen as a coherent syndrome
which was labelled PTSD. This is largely a phenomenological
classification. Aetiology is formulated in terms of a traumatic event
outside the range of usual human experience. It was this very
definition of PTSD as a 'normal reaction to an abnormal situation'
that caused some practitioners to doubt whether it is a psychiatric
disorder at all (see O'Donohue and Elliot, 1992).

There is, however, sound evidence that exposure to extreme, acute
stress does increase psychiatric morbidity (Raphael, 1986). Various
studies of different kinds of disaster indicate that one year after the
trauma, some 30–40 per cent of survivors manifested significant
psychological impairment, the level of morbidity reducing only slowly
over the next five years.

The defininition of PTSD in adults is the development of particular
symptoms following a distressing event *outside the range of usual human
experience*. These symptoms can include: persistent re-experiencing
of stimuli associated with the trauma and a variety of signs of increased
physiological arousal (for example, difficulties in concentration and
sleep disturbance).

The difficulty that arises with the notion that PTSD is a normal reaction to an abnormal situation is that we are unable to adequately operationalize the criteria for specifying which stressors are outside the range of usual/normal human experience. The trauma giving rise to PTSD seem to be those which violate the individual's safety assumptions more than events leading to other forms of anxiety, and there is far more re-experiencing of the traumatic event. It is this internal subjective experience that appears particularly to mark out PTSD from other disorders (see Jones and Barlow, 1992).

# Part I: Assessment

## Key criteria for the diagnosis of PTSD

The key criteria are as follows:

1.    The existence of a recognizable stressor that would evoke significant symptoms of distress in almost everyone.

2.    Re-experiencing the trauma as evidenced by at least **one** of the following:
    *    recurrent intrusive recollections of the event;
    *    recurrent dreams of the event;
    *    suddenly acting or feeling as if the traumatic event were recurring, because of an association with an environmental stimulus or mental reminder.

3.    Numbing of responsiveness to, or reduced involvement with, the external world, beginning some time after the trauma, and shown by at least **one** of the following:
    *    markedly diminished interest in one or more significant activities;
    *    feelings of detachment or estrangement from others;
    *    constricted affect (that is, inability to experience feelings).

4.    At least **two** of the following symptoms that were not present before the trauma:
    *    hyperalertness or exaggerated startle response;
    *    sleep disturbance;
    *    guilt about surviving when others have not, or about behaviours which were required for survival;
    *    memory impairment or trouble concentrating;
    *    avoidance of activities which arouse recollection of the traumatic event;
    *    intensification of symptoms by exposure to events that symbolize or resemble the traumatic event.

If a person meets some, but not the major criteria, then it would be more correct to say that they have a post-traumatic stress *reaction*, rather than the disorder. Bereavement, chronic illness, or marital conflict would not constitute the defining traumatic events, as they are not thought of as being outside the range of common experience.

## PTSD in childhood

Unfortunately, there are relatively few systematic investigations of the effects of major trauma in children and those that have been published tend to suffer from methodological weaknesses (see Garmezy, 1986).

It is worth looking at Yule's description of one of the major disasters involving children, the sinking of the cruise ship *Jupiter* (Yule, 1991). It led to a valuable study of the effects on children's fears, depression and anxiety (Yule, Udwin and Murdoch, 1990). On 21st October, 1988, the *Jupiter* sailed from Athens to take a party of around 400 British school children and their teachers on an educational cruise of the eastern Mediterranean. As they left harbour, it was beginning to get dark. Some of the groups were lining up for the evening meal, some were attending a briefing lecture on what they were to see on the trip. Just out of the harbour, the *Jupiter* was struck amidships by an Italian tanker and holed.

At first, no one realized the seriousness of their predicament, but very quickly the *Jupiter* shipped water and began listing badly to the port and aft. Children were told to assemble in a lounge on an upper deck, but many were unfamiliar with the layout of the ship. As the vessel listed at 45 degrees and then worse, they found it very difficult to move. Children became separated from friends and teachers. Many were able to jump across to tugs that had come alongside, but sadly two seamen assisting in the transfer were fatally crushed between the ship and the tug. Many children saw their dead bodies.

Other children, some of whom were non-swimmers, clung to the railings on the topmost deck under the lifeboats and had to jump in the water as the *Jupiter* went down, its funnel hissing and spurting out soot and smoke. Children and staff clung to wreckage in the dark oily water until rescued. Some of those swimming in the water were terrified lest they were run down by the rescue craft, and it was many hours before it was realized that all but one child and one teacher had survived. After spending a sleepless night on a sister ship moored in Piraeus harbour, the children were flown back to the UK to a barrage of publicity the next day. Althought the tour company offered to arrange counselling for any of the children who requested it, schools varied enormously in how they dealt with the aftermath. Some were very sympathetic and arranged individual and group help; others wanted to forget the whole episode and discouraged children from even talking about it (Yule, 1991).

Yule and his colleagues asked all fourth year girls in one school which had had a party of 24 aboard the *Jupiter* to complete the *Revised Fear Survey Schedule for Children*. Effectively, there were three subgroups of girls – those who went on the cruise and were traumatized, those who had wanted to go but could not get a place, and those who showed no interest in going in the first place. However, this latter group could not be considered as an unaffected control group as the whole school was badly affected by the aftermath of the disaster. Accordingly, fourth year girls in a nearby school also completed the fear schedule, along with the depression and anxiety scales.

The girls who had been on the cruise were significantly more depressed and anxious than the other groups five months after the disaster. Eleven of the fear items were judged to be related to the sinking and 33 were unrelated. There were no differences across the four exposure groups on unrelated fears. By contrast, on related fears, only the girls who experienced the traumatic events showed a significant increase in reported fears. Thus, the effects of the disaster on children's fears are specific to stimuli present and this provides more confirmatory evidence of the conditioning theory of fear acquisition (see Yule, Udwin and Murdoch, 1990). I will return to this study later on.

## Symptoms manifested in children

The *Jupiter* and other studies provide evidence that children and teenagers who survive a life-threatening disaster display most of the same range of symptoms as do adults.

Most children suffering from PTSD are troubled by:

➤ repetitive, intrusive thoughts about the event (this can happen at any time, particularly in quiet periods, such as bedtime or when reminders occur);

➤ vivid flashbacks;

➤ sleep disturbances (particularly in the first few weeks) brought about by fears of the dark, bad dreams, nightmares, and waking throughout the night;

➤ separation difficulties (even among adolescents) – not letting parents out of sight; sleeping in the parental bed;

➤ anger and irritability, being on a 'short fuse' with parents and peers;

➤ difficulty talking to peers and parents (not wishing to upset them or peers not wishing to upset the survivor);

➤ parental unawareness of their suffering;

➤ cognitive changes such as difficulties in concentrating, especially at school;

➤ memory problems in mastering/remembering new and old skills;

➤ incessant alertness to possible dangers in their environment;

➤ a sense of the fragility of life (pessimism, loss of faith, feeling that the future is foreshortened);

➤ changed priorities (for example not planning ahead);

➤ changes in values (this could be positive);

➤ fears associated with specific aspects of the traumatic situation;

➤ avoidance of situations associated with specific aspects of the traumatic situation;

➤ survivor guilt;

➤ depression (notably in adolescents), suicidal thoughts;

➤ panic attacks.

## Effects on very young children

Clinically, there is general agreement that preschool children react differently to major stressful experiences. Very young children have only a limited understanding of the life-threatening nature of disasters, but there is evidence that some preschool children have very adult concepts of dying and death (see *Appendix II*). The child's ability, early in life, to process information emotionally and cognitively, is essential to adaptation. Children over 28 months who are traumatized often demonstrate impressive, detailed and accurate verbal memory of the events. Repetitive play or drawings about the events are quite common in preschool children. Visual memories seem imprinted vividly in memory store and these comments gave rise to re-enactments in behaviour (Terr, 1988). Younger children may manifest a variety of regressive or antisocial behaviours at home and at school.

## Assessment measures

There are various methods suitable for identifying post-traumatic reactions in children (see Finch and Daugherty, 1993; Yule and Udwin, 1991). For example:

> ➤ **The Children's Stress Reaction Index** (Frederick and Pynoos, 1988).
> ➤ **Revised Impact of Events Scale** (Horowitz *et al.*, 1979).
> ➤ **Children's Post-traumatic Stress Disorder Inventory** (Saigh, 1989).

There is a need for specially developed semistructured interviews to discover the unique aspects of the particular trauma or disaster for each individual survivor (see Pynoos and Eth, 1986).

## Prevalence

To give an idea of the relative prevalence of the different symptoms, Yule (1994a) presented the findings from a study of over 100 adolescents who were clinically assessed following the sinking of the *Jupiter* cruise ship. As can be seen in Table 1, the most common symptoms within this sample included intrusive thoughts, distress at exposures to reminders, and avoidance of things associated with the disaster. Some 40–60 per cent showed evidence of increased physiological arousal, while many fewer showed emotional numbing or flashbacks.

**Table 1.** Prevalence of post-traumatic stress disorder symptoms in survivors of the *Jupiter* sinking

| PTSD individual items | No | Yes |
|---|---|---|
| Recurrent, intrusive thoughts | 25.6 | 74.4 |
| Recurrent dreams | 64.4 | 35.6 |
| Flashbacks | 80.0 | 15.6 |
| Distress at exposure | 24.4 | 74.4 |
| Avoids thoughts/feelings | 31.1 | 65.6 |
| Avoids activities | 27.8 | 71.1 |
| Amnesia | 68.9 | 28.9 |
| Loss of interest | 43.3 | 54.4 |
| Feelings of detachment | 51.1 | 42.2 |
| Restricted affect | 80.0 | 8.9 |
| Foreshortened future | 84.4 | 7.8 |
| Sleep difficulties | 48.9 | 51.1 |
| Irritability, anger | 41.1 | 58.9 |
| Poor concentration | 35.6 | 63.3 |
| Hypervigilance | 55.6 | 40.0 |
| Exaggerated startle | 38.9 | 51.1 |
| Physiological reactivity | 45.6 | 51.0 |

# Developmental variations

Although there are developmentally-based differences in the manifestation of symptoms and in the pattern of disorder between children and adults, such variations would not appear to justify the use of separate diagnostic criteria for children. The adult criteria described earlier are generally speaking adequate in describing the response to trauma in children. Nevertheless, modifications have been introduced in a later version of the DSM which more particularly describe possible reactions in children:

➢   Children may re-experience the trauma by means of repetitive playing out of themes derived from the traumatic event.

➢   There may be the loss of recently acquired developmental skills – a child might regress to an earlier maturational level.

➢   Children may experience a marked change in orientation to the future. This change in attitude may show itself in a sense of a foreshortened future; that is, the child does not expect to achieve the usual goals of career, family, or even of reaching adulthood.

➢   The disturbance in future orientation might also include what is referred to as 'omen formation', or the false belief in an ability to prophesy future catastrophic events.

➢   Symptoms such as the onset of new fears or the recurrence of old ones, somatic complaints, accidents and reckless behaviour merit consideration, given that these components are found to be associated with a PTSD diagnosis in severely affected children.

## Precipitants

According to the DSM, PTSD may be precipitated by three forms of traumatic stress:

➢   the direct experience of threat to oneself;

➢   the observation of harm to others;

➢   learning about a serious threat or harm to a close friend or relative.

PTSD has been reported in children who have been the victims of war; in children who have been the victims of sexual abuse; in children who have witnessed the abuse of their parents; in children who have survived natural disaster; in children who have survived the loss of a parent or sibling to accidental death or murder; and in children who have witnessed or survived accidents.

The precipitating events may be discrete (a one-off disaster) or a continuing series of trauma. They may be transmitted verbally, a form of vicarious traumatizing.

## Vulnerability factors

There are marked differences in the vulnerability of children exposed to the stresses of everyday life. In the face of life-threatening disasters the range of differences narrows, but there remains a degree of variability of response. For example, young people whose lives are at greatest risk are most likely to suffer extreme stress reactions, and the same applies to those who witness death and carnage. The strongest predictors of the numbers of symptoms are the overall level of functioning of the child's parents and the supportive (or unstable) nature and atmosphere in the home. (An assessment of parental functioning would seem to be critical for determining which children are most likely to be at risk.)

Children who are less able intellectually are particularly at risk. Another difference in vulnerability is gender-based: there is a higher proportion of problems among girls than among boys.

# Persistence of PTSD symptoms

There is a paucity of follow-up studies of PTSD. However, we know that the initial levels of distress experienced following a disaster are strongly related to later events. The more severe the trauma, the more probable it is that effects will last for six months to a year, or longer. Many problems simply do not resolve spontaneously. It is risky to be too philosophical, as one tends to be with the age-related fears of childhood. The phrase 'Oh s/he will grow out of it (or 'get over it')' is not necessarily the prognosis with PTSD.

Galante and Foa (1986) examined children initially at six months and then at 18 months after an earthquake disaster. Significant numbers of children still presented with at-risk symptoms at 18 months; in one village, the percentage of at-risk scores had actually increased significantly. McFarlane *et al.* (1987) and Earls *et al.* (1988) similarly found persistent effects evident at 26 months and 12 months respectively subsequent to the precipitating traumatic event. The persistence of PTSD symptoms in children potentially denies them the opportunity to enjoy, or benefit from, growth-promoting experiences.

A key issue is thought to be the child's capacity to remember a traumatic event. Psychological trauma are postulated to depend on a memory trace being formed: if the event does not register in consciousness and memory, then it cannot traumatize (Terr, 1988).

## The perception of disturbance

An important issue in the assessment of the symptoms of PTSD in young children is the validity of parental (or teacher) report as opposed to the child's self-report. Some studies have relied exclusively on adult perceptions of children's disturbance (for example, Galante and Foa, 1986) whereas other studies have relied on self-report (for example, Yule and Udwin, 1991). However, it would appear that parents and other adults (notably teachers) when interviewed often fail to report children's problems, because they tend to under-estimate the effects of disasters and the level of distress experienced by child survivors. They may also estimate children's distress differently.

## Causal factors

Yule (1994b) makes the point that it is not known whether PTSD differs from other recognized psychological disorders precipitated by various life stresses such as parental conflict and separation, in degree or kind. Similarly, there is no evidence whether genetic factors play a role in vulnerability to PTSD or, if they do, whether they are the same as those that predispose to anxiety or affective disorders.

# Part II: Treatment and counselling

Sadly, relatively little (although not too little to leave health professionals pessimistic or helpless) is known about treating child survivors. In the immediate aftermath of a trauma, children usually need to be reunited with their parents and family. Teenagers as well as younger survivors may wish to sleep in their parents' bed. The professional's first task is to help parents to understand the nature of PTSD and thus mobilize their tolerance, patience and reassurance. All may be needed! We do know that parental involvement in treatment is a vital component of sucess (Deblinger *et al.*, 1990).

## Re-exposure

The other core component in virtually all formal treatment strategies has been some form of *re-exposure* to the traumatic cues, conducted in a structured and supportive manner (Lyons, 1987). Activities such as semi-structured art activities, writing, storytelling, music, and puppetry are all thought to be useful, particularly with younger children, as activities which facilitate the process of re-exposure.

Such activities can occur spontaneously in children's play and may well form the basis of developmentally appropriate styles of coping, especially when they take place in the context of a supportive family.

## Crisis intervention debriefing

The technique called *Critical Incident Stress Debriefing* has been adapted for use with children (see Dyregrov, 1988; 1991). The following précis description is taken from Yule (1994b).

Soon after an incident (within a few days) the survivors are brought together in a group with an outside facilitator/leader who formulates the rules for the introductory meeting. The goals are to share feelings and help each other in a context of privacy and confidentiality. No one is required to talk, although all are encouraged to participate. No teasing of other children must follow the gleaning of information.

Next, there is a clarification of the facts concerning what actually occurred during the traumatic events; this helps to reduce the rumours that surround such incidents. Group members are asked what they thought when they realized something was wrong. This moves the discussion on to how the children felt at the time and to their current emotional reactions. Children can thus share the variety of feelings they have experienced and learn, and often get comfort, from the similarity of the emotions and reactions experienced by their fellow survivors. The leader labels their reactions as normal and understandable responses to an abnormal situation, and the children often feel relief that their strange feelings (for example, symptoms of PTSD) are not signs of madness. The leader summarizes the information that emerges from the group discussion and educates the children with regard to simple strategies (such as deep, slow breathing, muscular and mental relaxation, thought stopping and distraction) they can adopt in order to control some of the reactions. They are informed about other sources of help that are available should their distress persist or increase.

Yule (1994b) cautions that given the few evaluative studies of debriefing, and the assumption that individuals will adapt to crises at different rates, care must be exercised before offering debriefing as a panacea to all survivors. Nevertheless, the importance of debriefing and its efficacy in alleviating the stress that follows a disaster seems to be widely accepted (Blom, Etkind and Carr, 1991) although the efficacy of debriefing procedures has yet to be established empirically. As we saw earlier, Yule and Udwin (1991) worked with 24 girls who had survived the sinking of the *Jupiter* in 1988. The girls were assessed and debriefed ten days afterwards and then further assessed five months later, using the same instruments. Scores on the *Impact of Events Scale* remained high and revealed that they were still experiencing unpleasant and intrusive thoughts about the incident. Scores on both the anxiety and depression scales had significantly increased.

## To talk or not to talk?

It is difficult to know what to say and when to say it when a child has suffered a personal tragedy. Should things be left well alone if a child is reluctant to talk? There are no easy answers. Each case must be judged on its merits, its special circumstances. When a child is bereaved by a disaster, no treatment plan can ignore his or her grief. Yule (1994b) makes the point that it is advisable to get children to repeat back to you what you have tried to explain, so that muddles or misunderstandings can be ironed out.

### Normalizing

Like adults, children (and especially adolescents) worry that they are going mad when they begin to experience PTSD symptoms. They should be reassured about the normality of their feelings.

## Individual treatment

### What you feel, think and do

As the counsellor, you might say to the child, taking their feelings as your lead:

➤ **Sudden feelings** – you may feel as if the traumatic event were happening again; this may just come over you when some sort of reminder occurs.

➤ **Intrusive thoughts and images about the event** – these thoughts and pictures of the circumstances may force themselves into your mind even when you don't want them to. The pictures and thoughts may be very vivid and it may feel as though the event is happening all over again even with sensations like sound and smell being experienced. Re-experiencing like this is common even though it is very distressing and frightening.

➤ **Feeling nothing much at all** – you may surprise yourself, or other people, because you can't feel very much at all about anything. You may seem just numb, as if anaesthetized.

➤ **Feeling detached from other people** – you may find it difficult to respond or behave normally with other people. You may find you feel almost cut off or isolated from others, even from those you love or know well. It can feel very odd and uncomfortable.

➤ **Guilt feelings** – if you have been in an incident where others did not survive or where others were injured more severely than you, you may later suffer from intense feelings of guilt. You may feel *you* should have died, or that it was not fair that others were more severely injured. You may wish you had acted differently in some way at the time. Your feelings and thoughts may not make sense, but in spite of that they can affect you quite powerfully.

➤ **Difficulty in concentrating and remembering** – difficulties here can make us feel angry or very worried: you may think you are 'losing your mind'. Poor memory and poor concentration can last for quite some time after a traumatic event.

➤ **Feeling jittery** – you may find yourself behaving as though you are very much on edge, or jittery. You may find yourself being startled by noises, even quiet ones, or by people coming in and out when you aren't expecting them.

➤ **A tendency to avoid reminders of the event** – you may notice that even some time after the event, you are avoiding doing things or going to certain places, because those things remind you of the event. These avoidances can be protective and helpful for a while, but counterproductive or unhelpful later on.

➤ **Sleeping badly** – you may find it difficult to get off to sleep or you may find you keep waking up, especially if you are suffering from nightmares. If you have woken up it may be impossible to get back to sleep.

➤ **Feelings and behaviour being 'triggered' by what we see and hear** – we cannot always protect ourselves from chance reminders of what was a traumatic event for us. News reports on TV and in the papers, pictures and conversations, can be avoided to begin with, but these and all sorts of other things can trigger memories and bring back problems such as lack of sleep.

## Some ideas to help and support the child

➤ Make opportunities for conversation while sharing an activity or playing. Talking while playing, doing a craft activity or drawing with the child is a way of being close and comforting.

➤ Ask the child how *they* would like support.

➤ Let him or her know it's alright to feel peculiar, afraid, angry or guilty.

➤ Use books/stories/music to distract and calm the child, especially at night when they are thinking thoughts that make them afraid.

➤ Give time and attention: *listen* (see Ward *et al.*, 1993).

➤ Tackle the taboo subjects: be honest with questions.

➤ Watch for verbalizations and behaviour changes that suggest particular problems (for example, fear, guilt, depression).

➤ Involve the child's special friends in visits. Discourage social isolation.

➤ Provide the occasional opportunity for privacy, a place for the child to express emotions or be quietly alone.

# Ways to help families come to terms with the child's PTSD

The family may need help:

➤ to accept and understand the child's difficulties;
➤ to express their feelings/emotions;
➤ to accept their child's feelings as normal;
➤ to deal with 'tasks' that families have to get on with in life;
➤ to clarify distortions and misconceptions;
➤ to cope with family changes.

# Helping siblings and parents

➤ Encourage 'healing family tasks'. This implies:
  • a shared knowledge of the reality of a traumatic experience and its aftermath;
  • reorganization of the family system where a child is permanently disabled or there has been a death of one of the family members.

# Some dos for the counsellor

➤ Be available to the family; keep in touch.

➤ Listen – give permission to them to express as much of their shock and sadness as they are willing to share at the time.

➤ Encourage them to talk about their feelings and concerns.

➤ Normalize family feelings; accept them; explain them (if necessary).

➤ Be honest and open with questions. Say 'I don't know' when you don't know the answer.

➤ Ask parents/children what help/support they would like.

## Some don'ts for the counsellor

➤ Don't advise family members not to worry or not to be sad.

➤ Don't advise them as to what they *should* feel or do.

➤ Don't say you *know* how they feel – you don't!

➤ Don't say 'You should be feeling better now'.

➤ Don't say 'At least you are still alive'.

➤ Don't encourage parents to hide their feelings from their child.

➤ Don't neglect to liaise with the school. Children when traumatized may 'misbehave' ('act out') and/or underachieve due to poor concentration, apathy or low motivation (as part of a feeling of depression). Teachers may not be fully aware of the reason for this behaviour.

## Some dos and don'ts for the parent

(See also *Hints for Parents*.)

➤ Do allow children (if bereaved) to go through their own individual stages of grief.

➤ Do seek help from other supportive persons.

➤ Do notify the child's school or day care centre about the child's trauma.

➤ Do consider trauma counselling/support groups for children if available.

➤ Do provide continued assurance of love and support, and when words fail, touch.

LIVERPOOL
JOHN MOORES UNIVERSITY
AVRIL ROBARTS LRC
TITHEBARN STREET
LIVERPOOL L2 2ER
TEL. 0151 231 4022

> Don't discourage the subject of the disaster in the home.

> Don't discourage the emotions of grief and shock.

> Don't speak beyond a child's level of comprehension.

## Some dos for the child

> *Do* talk about what has happened to you if you can, particularly to those adults who are looking after you or who love you. Do not feel that you *have* to do so. You may find you can say only a bit at a time; that you do not wish to talk further. If this happens then *say so*.

> *Do* accept sadness and crying as normal particularly in the early stages of shock, although you may not like it.

> *Do* try to control your fear or panic by whatever means you know, by relaxation, distraction, talking to people, thinking about other things.

## Some don'ts for the child

> *Don't* avoid showing your feelings. You may be experiencing a mixture of powerful emotions: grief, anger, sadness, guilt, fear, relief, hope.

> *Don't* be surprised if your emotions go up and down.

> *Don't* expect bad memories to vanish. They are normal. The task is to manage your thoughts by putting them out of mind, by distracting yourself, and (in the first instance) in telling yourself that what is happening to you is normal and only to be expected. In this way memories become less of a problem.

# References

American Psychiatric Association (1987). *Diagnostic and Statistical Manual of Mental Disorders* (3rd ed. rev.) Washington D.C.: American Psychiatric Press.

Applebaum, D.R. and Burns, G.L. (1991). Unexpected childhood death: Post-traumatic stress disorder in surviving siblings and parents. *Journal of Clinical Child Psychology, 20,* 114–120.

Blom, G.E., Etkind, S.L. and Carr, W.J. (1991). Psychological interventions after child and adolescent disasters in the community. *Child Psychiatry and Human Development, 21,* 257–266.

Brett, E.A., Spitzer, R.L. and Williams, J.B.W. (1988). DSM-III-R criteria for post-traumatic stress disorder. *American Journal of Psychiatry, 145,* 1232–1236.

Clunies-Ross, C. and Lansdowne, R. (1988). Concepts of death, illness and isolation found in children with leukaemia. *Child Care, Health and Development, 14,* 373–386.

Deblinger, E., McLeer, S. and Henry, H. (1990). Cognitive behavioural treatment for sexually abused children suffering post-traumatic stress: Preliminary findings. *Journal of the American Academy of Child and Adolescent Psychiatry, 29,* 747–752.

Dyregrov, A. (1988). *Critical Incident Stress Debriefings.* Research Centre for Occupational Health and Safety, University of Bergen, Norway. Unpublished document.

Dyregrov, A. (1991). *Grief in Children: A Handbook for Adults.* London: Jessica Kingsley.

Earls, F., Smith, E., Reich, W. and Jung K.G. (1988). Investigating psychopathological consequences of a disaster in children: A pilot study incorporating a structured diagnostic interview. *Journal of the American Academy of Child and Adolescent Psychiatry, 27,* 90–95.

Finch, A.J. and Daugherty, T.K. (1993). Issues in the assessment of post-traumatic disorder in children. In: C.F. Saylor (Ed.) *Children and Disasters.* New York: Plenum Press.

Frederick, C.J. and Pynoos, R.S. (1988). *The Child Post-Traumatic Stress Disorder (PTSD) Reaction Index.* Los Angeles: University of California.

Galante, R. and Foa, D. (1986). An epidemiological study of psychic trauma and treatment effectiveness for children after natural disaster. *Journal of the American Academy of Child and Adolescent Psychiatry, 25,* 357–363.

Garmezy, N. (1986). Children under severe stress: Critique and comments. *Journal of the American Academy of Child Psychiatry, 25,* 384–392.

Hopkins, O. and King, N. (1995). Post-traumatic stress disorder in children and adolescents. *Behaviour Change, 11,* 72–120.

Horowitz, M.J., Wilner, N. and Alvarez, W. (1979). Impact of Events Scale: A measure of subjective stress. *Psychosomatic Medicine, 41,* 209–218.

Jones, J.C. and Barlow, D.H. (1992). A new model for post-traumatic stress disorder: implications for the future. In: P.A. Saigh (Ed.) *Post-traumatic Stress Disorder: A Behavioural Approach to Assessment and Treatment.* New York: MacMillan.

Kane, B (1979). Children's concepts of death. *Journal of Genetic Psychology, 134,* 141–145.

Lyons, J.A. (1987). Post-traumatic stress disorder in children and adolescents. A review of the literature. *Developmental and Behavioural Paediatrics, 8,* 349–356.

McFarlane, A.C., Policansky, S.K. and Irwin, C. (1987). A longitudinal study of the psychological morbidity in children due to a natural disaster. *Psychological Medicine, 17,* 727–738.

O'Donohue, W. and Eliot, A (1992). The current status of post-traumatic stress disorder as a diagnostic category: problems and proposals. *Journal of Traumatic Stress, 5,* 421–439.

Pynoos, R.S. and Eth, S. (1986). Witness to violence: the child interview. *Journal of the American Academy of Child Psychiatry, 25,* 306–319.

Raphael, B. (1986). *When Disaster Strikes: A Handbook for the Caring Professions.* London: Hutchinson.

Saigh, P.A. (1989). The development and validation of the Children's Post-traumatic Stress Disorder Inventory. *International Journal of Special Education, 4,* 75–84.

Terr, L. (1988). What happens to early memories of trauma? *Journal of the American Academy of Child and Adolescent Psychiatry, 27,* 96–104.

Terr, L. (1991). Childhood traumas – an outline and overview. *American Journal of Psychiatry, 148,* 10–20.

Ward, B. and Associates (1993). *Good Grief: Exploring Feelings, Loss and Death with Under Elevens.* London: Jessica Kingsley Publishers.

Yule, W. (1991). Work with children following disasters. In M. Herbert, *Clinical Child Psychology: Social Learning, Development and Behaviour.* Chichester: Wiley.

Yule, W. (1994a). Post-traumatic stress disorder. In: T.H. Ollendick, N.J. King and W. Yule (Eds) *International Handbook of Phobic and Anxiety Disorders in Children and Adolescents.* New York: Plenum Press.

Yule, W. (1994b). Post-traumatic stress disorder. In M. Rutter, E. Taylor and L. Hersov (Eds) *Child and Adolescent Psychiatry.* Oxford: Blackwell Scientific Publications.

Yule, W. and Udwin, O. (1991). Screening child survivors for post-traumatic stress disorders. *British Journal of Clinical Psychology, 30,* 1051–1061.

Yule, W., Udwin, O. and Murdoch, K. (1990). The 'Jupiter' sinking: effects on children's fears, depression and anxiety. *Journal of Child Psycyhology and Psychiatry, 31,* 1051–1061.

A useful guide for schools is *Wise Before the Event: Coping with Crises in Schools.* W. Yule and Anne Gold. London: Calouste Gulbenkian Foundation, 1993.

# Appendix I: ICD-10 and DSM-IV Criteria for PTSD

## ICD-10: Post-traumatic Stress Disorder

As stated in ICD-10 (World Health Organization, 1992), PTSD arises as a delayed or protracted response to a stressful event or situation of an exceptionally threatening or catastrophic nature, which is likely to cause pervasive distress in almost everyone.

## DSM-IV criteria for Post-traumatic Stress Disorder

**A.** The person has been exposed to a traumatic event in which both of the following have been present:
1. The person has experienced, witnessed, or been confronted with an event or events that involve actual or threatened death or serious injury, or a threat to the physical integrity of oneself or others.
2. The person's response involved intense fear, helplessness, or horror. Note: In children, it may be expressed instead by disorganized or agitated behaviour.

**B.** The traumatic event is persistently re-experienced in at least one of the following ways:
1. Recurrent and intrusive distressing recollections of the event, including images, thoughts, or perceptions. Note: In young children, repetitive play may occur in which themes or aspects of the trauma are expressed.
2. Recurrent distressing dreams of the event. Note: In children, there may be frightening dreams without recognizable content.
3. Acting or feeling as if the traumatic event were recurring (includes a sense of reliving the experience, illusions, hallucinations, and dissociative flashback episodes, including those that occur upon awakening or when intoxicated). Note: In young children, trauma-specific re-enactment may occur.

4.    Intense psychological distress at exposure to internal or external cues that symbolize or resemble an aspect of the traumatic event.

5.    Physiological reactivity upon exposure to internal or external cues that symbolize or resemble an aspect of the traumatic event.

C.    Persistent avoidance of stimuli associated with the trauma and numbing of general responsiveness (not present before the trauma), as indicated by at least three of the following:

1.    Efforts to avoid thoughts, feelings, or conversations associated with the trauma.

2.    Efforts to avoid activities, places, or people that arouse recollections of the trauma.

3.    Inability to recall an important aspect of the trauma.

4.    Markedly diminished interest or participation in significant activities.

5.    Feeling of detachment or estrangement from others.

6.    Restricted range of affect (e.g. unable to have loving feelings).

7.    Sense of a foreshortened future (e.g. does not expect to have a career, marriage, children, or a normal life span).

D.    Persistent symptoms of increased arousal (not present before the trauma), as indicated by at least two of the following:

1.    Difficulty falling or staying asleep.

2.    Irritability or outbursts of anger.

3.    Difficulty concentrating.

4.    Hypervigilance.

5.    Exaggerated startle response.

E.    Duration of the disturbance (symptoms in B, C, and D) is more than 1 month.

F.    The disturbance causes clinically significant distress or impairment in social, occupational, or other important areas of functioning.

*Specify if:*

*Acute:* If duration of symptoms is less than three months.
*Chronic:* If duration of symptoms is three months or more.

*Specify if:*

*With delayed onset:* Onset of symptoms at least 6 months after the stressor.

# Appendix II: Development of the concept of death

The way in which children make sense of (or fail to comprehend) death and grief is related to their cognitive, emotional and physical stages of development. The information following (see Kane, 1979) is based on empirical studies; that is, it is based upon generalizations to which there are exceptions, especially with regard to differences in life-experience and individual differences in the rate of development.

## Children under 4 years of age

### 1. Cognitive factors

➤ The 'preconceptual stage' of cognitive development lasts from about two to four years of age. At this stage children's concepts are not fully formed. They don't understand, for example, the permanence of death. Because their thinking is prelogical and often 'magical' (the notion that some things and people have power over others; also the child experiencing him/herself as at the centre of things), misconceptions and misinterpretations of the 'world' they live in can be a problem. Another source of worry to the child is their misinterpretation of causality. The immature kind of thinking called 'psychological causality' refers to the tendency in young children to attribute a **psychological motive** as the cause of events. For example, children may think that a parent has gone to hospital because he or she is angry with them, rather than due to illness.

➤ Distress on separation implies attachment to the person. The mean age of the onset of attachment is in the third quarter of the first year (notably 6–8 months).

➤ Very young children (most three-year-olds and even younger children) are aware of death and are familiar with the word 'death' before they enter school.

➤ Their ability to conceptualize death and its implications is very limited. For example, because they do not understand that death is final, they may search for the departed parent and pester the surviving one ('When is Mummy/Daddy coming back?').

➤ Children develop a realistic concept of death gradually; new components of understanding are 'added in' so as eventually to bring about a full grasp of its realities.

## 2. Emotional factors

➤ At this early stage, children's emotional reactions to the disappearance of a parent, for whatever cause, tend to be similar. Children of barely four years of age can yearn for departed parents, and wait for their return.

➤ Children older than a few weeks or months display the same separation anxiety whether the parent is away for a few hours or for considerably longer.

➤ Young children cannot sustain a sad mood for prolonged periods of time.

➤ They cannot differentiate feelings as finely as older children.

## 3. Physical factors

➤ Children who are too young to make themselves understood through speech may react physically to the bereavement by:
- wetting
- loss of appetite
- disturbed sleep
- clinging behaviour
- catching infections

# Children aged 5–10 years

## 1. Cognitive factors

➤ The **intuitive** stage of thinking (4–7 years) moves the child on from the preconceptual stage (2–4) mentioned earlier, and they develop the ability to classify, order and quantify things, but they are still unaware of the principles which underlie these abilities. It is only in the next stage of *concrete operations* (7 plus) that these principles become more explicit, so that children can explain their logical reasoning in a satisfactory way.

➢    Before the age of 6 or 7 children often attribute life to inanimate objects.

➢    It is between the ages of 7 and 9 that there appears to be a nodal point in children's development of concepts about life and death. By about 7 most children have a fairly clear idea of 'life' and a more or less complete concept of 'death'. It shouldn't be forgotten that many 5-year-olds have a fairly full concept.

➢    When children are about 8–9, they realize that dying can apply to themselves.

Kane (1979) describes the child's understanding of death between the ages of five and ten in terms of the components he or she is cognitively capable of comprehending, as follows:

➢    **Separation** (understood by most five-year-olds). Young children can be very aware that death means separation from their parents, friends or brothers and sisters. This may be the main concept they focus on, and they may be concerned that they will feel lonely or that their parents will be lonely without them.

➢    **Immobility** (understood by most five-year-olds). The awareness that dead people cannot move can concern some children who are not also aware that dead people cannot feel, see or hear.

➢    **Irrevocability** (understood by most six-year-olds). The fact that once people die they cannot come back to life again is essential in understanding death. Many children younger than five or six may not realize the finality of the process. Children play games at being shot and dying, but then leap to life the next minute. 'Pretend' death and 'real' death need to be made clear, so that the child realizes that 'real' death means never living again.

➢    **Causality** (understood by most six-year-olds). There is always a physical cause of death. Young children, however, often have unusual or 'magical' ideas about what causes death. For example, a nasty wish, saying something horrible or being naughty can sometimes be perceived as having caused illness or death. Children need to understand that it is not such imaginary events that cause death, but that something is wrong with the body and that is what causes people to die.

➢    **Dysfunctionality** (understood by most six-year-olds). Explanations about death to children should include the cessation of bodily functions, for example, that the body stops breathing, growing, seeing, hearing, thinking and feeling, and the heart stops beating.

Some children worry they might be able to hear what is happening to themselves but not be able to tell anyone.

➤ **Universality** (understood by most seven-year-olds). That every living organism dies at some time is important in understanding that everyone must die eventually. This idea can comfort some children who may believe that everyone lives forever and that it is unfair that they, or someone they are close to, are dying.

➤ **Insensitivity** (understood by most eight-year-olds). That a dead person cannot feel anything is often difficult for young children to understand. For example, if they walk on a grave they may wonder if they are 'hurting' the person under the ground. One way of helping a child who is dying in pain, or who has parents who have been in pain, is to help them to realize they will never feel pain again after death. (The conceptual development of children with a serious illness – leukaemia – is not overall significantly different from that of healthy children (Clunies-Ross and Lansdowne, 1988).)

## 2. Emotional factors

➤ Disturbances of emotion and behaviour are common. In one study, 50 per cent manifested problems such as school refusal, stealing and poor concentration one year after the loss of a parent, while 30 per cent displayed problems after two years.

## Adolescents

### 1. Cognitive factors

➤ Appearance of the dead is understood by most 12-year-olds: a dead body looks different to a living body, and children may be very interested in the physical characteristics of death. They can seem ghoulish sometimes in their desire for detailed descriptions of what a dead person looks like.

➤ Adolescents, like adults, realize the permanence of death and therefore tend to look for meanings: the big 'Why?' questions.

➤ The adolescent's thinking is flexible. He or she is capable of abstract thought, can hypothesize and work things out (such as principles) for themselves. Thus, they may have their own theories about death and question cherished beliefs about, say, the afterlife, in a way that dismays the surviving parent.

## 2. Emotional factors

> ➤ Adolescents express their grief more like adults.

> ➤ The developmental task of separating from parents may be delayed (particularly for eldest children or those who are the same sex as the deceased parent). The adolescent's search for identity may be influenced by his/her answers to the 'Why' questions referred to earlier.

> ➤ Some adolescents display an apparent lack of feeling or indifference owing (it is postulated) to conflicts between the drives toward independence and continuing dependence (referred to previously).

# Hints for Parents 1: What is post-traumatic stress disorder?

Many children experience several distressing reactions including anxiety, fear and depression following major emotional/physical upheavals (disasters, accidents). It is now appreciated that they may be suffering from symptoms of Post-traumatic Stress Disorder (PTSD), and that without treatment their disorder can persist over long periods of time. Such children may be troubled by some or all of the following symptoms:

➤ Repetitive, intrusive thoughts and recollections about the accident/trauma (at any time; particularly in quiet periods, for example, bedtime or when reminders occur). They are called intrusive because they 'intrude' into the child's consciousness despite being resisted.

➤ Vivid flashbacks (mental images or pictures of the traumatic event and its consequences).

➤ Sleep disturbances (particularly in the first few weeks) brought about by fears of the dark, bad dreams, nightmares, and waking throughout the night.

➤ Separation difficulties, such as not letting parents out of sight; sleeping in parent's bed.

➤ Anger and irritability – being on a 'short fuse' with parents and peers.

➤ Difficulty talking to peers and parents (not wishing to upset them or peers not wishing to upset the survivor).

➤ Difficulties in concentrating, especially at school.

➤ Memory problems in mastering/remembering new and old skills.

➤ Incessant alertness to possible dangers in their environment.

➤ A sense of the fragility of life (pessimism, loss of faith, feeling that the future is foreshortened).

➤ Changed priorities (for example, not planning ahead).

➤ Changes in values (this could be positive).

➤ Fears associated with specific aspects of the traumatic situation.

➤ Avoidance of situations associated with specific aspects of the traumatic situation.

➤ Survivor guilt because they (and not others) survived the trauma.
➤ Depression (notably in adolescents), suicidal thoughts.
➤ Panic attacks.

It is important to realize that post-traumatic stress disorder is a **normal** (although disturbing) reaction, that is to say a common reaction to a particular abnormal situation.

PTSD may be precipitated by three forms of traumatic stress:

➤ the direct experience of threat to oneself;
➤ the observation of harm to others
➤ learning about a serious threat or harm to a close friend or relative.

PTSD has been reported in children who have been the victims of war; also in children who have been the victims of sexual abuse; children who have witnessed the abuse of their parents; children who have survived natural disaster; children who have survived the loss of a sibling or parent to accidental death; children who have witnessed or survived accidents.

PACTS SERIES  •  BRITISH PSYCHOLOGICAL SOCIETY  •  PACTS SERIES  •  BRITISH PSYCHOLOGICAL SOCIETY

# Hints for Parents 2: How can my child be helped?

## Treating and counselling

### To talk or not to talk

It is difficult to know what to say and when to say it when a child has suffered a personal tragedy. Should things be left well alone if a child is reluctant to talk? There are no easy answers. Each case must be judged on its merits and its special circumstances.

The practitioner you seek help from is likely to discuss the following issues with you:

➤ **Normalizing**
Like adults, children (and especially adolescents) worry that they are going mad when they begin to experience PTSD symptoms. They should be reassured about the normality of their feelings.

➤ **Re-exposure**
The common feature in virtually all treatments is some form of **re-exposure** to the traumatic cues conducted in a gradual and supportive manner. Activities such as art activities, writing, story-telling, music, and puppetry are all thought to be useful, particularly with younger children, as activities which help gently and indirectly, the process of 're-exposure'.

### Crisis intervention: debriefing

The technique called *Critical Incident Stress Debriefing* has been adapted for use with children. Soon after an incident (within a few days) the survivors are brought together in a group with an outside facilitator/leader who formulates the rules for the introductory meeting. The goals are to share feelings and help each other in a context of privacy and confidentiality. No one is required to talk, although all are encouraged to participate. No teasing of other children must follow the gleaning of information.

Next, there is a clarification of the facts concerning what actually occurred during the traumatic events; this helps to reduce the rumours that surround such incidents. Group members are asked about their thoughts when they realized something was wrong. This moves the discussion on to how the children felt at the time and their current emotional reactions. Children thus share the variety of feelings they've experienced and learn (and often get comfort) from the similarity of the emotions and other reactions from their fellow survivors. The leader labels their reactions as normal and understandable responses to an abnormal situation. There is often relief that their strange feelings (for example, symptoms of PTSD) are not signs of madness. The leader summarizes the information and teaches children self-help strategies they can adopt in order to control some of their fearful reactions. They are informed about other sources of help that are available should their distress persist or increase.

## Some dos and don'ts for parents

➤ Do allow children (if bereaved) to go through their own individual stages of grief.
➤ Do seek help from other supportive persons.
➤ Do notify the child's school or day care centre about the child's trauma.
➤ Do consider trauma counselling/support groups for children if available.
➤ Do provide continued assurance of love and support (when words fail, touch).
➤ Don't discourage the subject of the disaster in the home.
➤ Don't discourage the emotions of grief and shock.
➤ Don't speak beyond a child's level of comprehension.

# Hints for Parents 3: Some dos and don't for the child

## Some dos for the child

> *Do* talk about what has happened to you if you can, particularly to those adults who are looking after you or who love you. Do not feel that you *have* to do so. You may find you can say only a bit at a time; that you do not wish to talk further. If this happens then *say so*.

> *Do* accept sadness and crying as normal particularly in the early stages of shock, although you may not like it.

> *Do* try to control your fear or panic by whatever means you know, by relaxation, distraction, talking to people, thinking about other things.

## Some don'ts for the child

> *Don't* avoid showing your feelings. You may be experiencing a mixture of powerful emotions: grief, anger, sadness, guilt, fear, relief, hope.

> *Don't* be surprised if your emotions go up and down.

> *Don't* expect bad memories to vanish. They are normal. The task is to manage your thoughts by putting them out of mind, by distracting yourself, and (in the first instance) in telling yourself that what is happening to you is normal and only to be expected. In this way memories become less of a problem.